EFFECTIVE INSTRUCTION
FOR STUDENTS
WITH
SPECIAL NEEDS

A Practical Approach to Special Education for Every Teacher

The Fundamentals of Special Education
A Practical Guide for Every Teacher

The Legal Foundations of Special Education
A Practical Guide for Every Teacher

Effective Assessment for Students With Special Needs
A Practical Guide for Every Teacher

Effective Instruction for Students With Special Needs
A Practical Guide for Every Teacher

*Working With Families and Community Agencies
    to Support Students With Special Needs*
A Practical Guide for Every Teacher

Public Policy, School Reform, and Special Education
A Practical Guide for Every Teacher

Teaching Students With Sensory Disabilities
A Practical Guide for Every Teacher

Teaching Students With Medical, Physical, and Multiple Disabilities
A Practical Guide for Every Teacher

Teaching Students With Learning Disabilities
A Practical Guide for Every Teacher

Teaching Students With Communication Disorders
A Practical Guide for Every Teacher

Teaching Students With Emotional Disturbance
A Practical Guide for Every Teacher

Teaching Students With Mental Retardation
A Practical Guide for Every Teacher

Teaching Students With Gifts and Talents
A Practical Guide for Every Teacher

EFFECTIVE INSTRUCTION FOR STUDENTS WITH SPECIAL NEEDS

A Practical Guide for Every Teacher

BOB ALGOZZINE
JIM YSSELDYKE

CORWIN PRESS
A SAGE Publications Company
Thousand Oaks, California

For information:

Corwin Press
A Sage Publications Company
2455 Teller Road
Thousand Oaks, California 91320
www.corwinpress.com

Sage Publications Ltd.
1 Oliver's Yard
55 City Road
London EC1Y 1SP
United Kingdom

Sage Publications India Pvt. Ltd.
B-42, Panchsheel Enclave
Post Box 4109
New Delhi 110 017 India

Printed in the United States of America

Library of Congress Cataloging-in-Publication Data

Algozzine, Robert.
Effective instruction for students with special needs: A practical guide for every teacher / Bob Algozzine and James E. Ysseldyke.
    p. cm.
Includes bibliographical references and index.
ISBN 1-4129-3944-5 (cloth)
ISBN 1-4129-3897-X (pbk.)
    1. Special education—United States. 2. Effective teaching—United States. 3. Special education teachers—Training of—United States.
    I. Ysseldyke, James E. II. Title.
LC3981.A66 2006
371.9'043—dc22

                                                        2005037820

This book is printed on acid-free paper.

06   07   08   09   10   9   8   7   6   5   4   3   2   1

Acquisitions Editor:	Kylee M. Liegl
Editorial Assistant:	Nadia Kashper
Production Editor:	Denise Santoyo
Copy Editor:	Colleen Brennan
Typesetter:	C&M Digitals (P) Ltd.
Indexer:	Kathy Paparchontis
Cover Designer:	Michael Dubowe

Contents

About
A Practical Approach to Special Education for Every Teacher

S pecial education means specially designed instruction for students with unique learning needs. Students receive special education for many reasons. Students with disabilities such as mental retardation, hearing impairments (including deafness), speech or language impairments, visual impairments (including blindness), emotional disturbance, orthopedic impairments, autism, traumatic brain injury, other health impairments, or specific learning disabilities are entitled to special education services. Students who are gifted and talented also receive special education. Special education services are delivered in many settings, including regular classes, resource rooms, and separate classes. The 13 books of this collection will help you teach students with disabilities and those with gifts and talents. Each book focuses on a specific area of special education and can be used individually or in conjunction with all or some of the other books. Six of the books provide the background and content knowledge you need in order to work effectively with all students with unique learning needs:

Book 1: The Fundamentals of Special Education

Book 2: The Legal Foundations of Special Education

Book 3: Effective Assessment for Students With Special Needs

Book 4: Effective Instruction for Students With Special Needs

Book 5: Working With Families and Community Agencies to Support Students With Special Needs

Book 6: Public Policy, School Reform, and Special Education

Seven of the books focus on teaching specific groups of students who receive special education:

Book 7:   Teaching Students With Sensory Disabilities

Book 8:   Teaching Students With Medical, Physical, and Multiple Disabilities

Book 9:   Teaching Students With Learning Disabilities

Book 10: Teaching Students With Communication Disorders

Book 11: Teaching Students With Emotional Disturbance

Book 12: Teaching Students With Mental Retardation

Book 13: Teaching Students With Gifts and Talents

All of the books in *A Practical Approach to Special Education for Every Teacher* will help you to make a difference in the lives of all students, especially those with unique learning needs.

ACKNOWLEDGMENTS

The approach we take in *A Practical Approach to Special Education for Every Teacher* is an effort to change how professionals learn about special education. The 13 separate books are a result of prodding from our students and from professionals in the field to provide a set of materials that "cut to the chase" in teaching them about students with disabilities and about building the capacity of systems to meet those students' needs. Teachers told us that in their classes they always confront students with special learning needs and students their school district has assigned a label to (e.g., students with learning disabilities). Our students and the professionals we worked with wanted a very practical set of texts that gave them the necessary **information** *about* **the students** (e.g., federal definitions, student characteristics) and specific **information on** *what to do about* **the students** (assessment and teaching strategies, approaches that work). They also wanted the opportunity to purchase parts of textbooks, rather than entire texts, to learn what they needed.

The production of this collection would not have been possible without the support and assistance of many colleagues. Professionals associated with Corwin Press—Faye Zucker, Kylee Liegl, Robb Clouse—helped us work through the idea of introducing special education differently, and their support in helping us do it is deeply appreciated.

Faye Ysseldyke and Kate Algozzine, our children, and our grandchildren also deserve recognition. They have made the problems associated with the project very easy to diminish, deal with, or dismiss. Every day in every way, they enrich our lives and make us better. We are grateful for them.

About the Authors

Bob Algozzine, PhD, is professor in the Department of Educational Leadership at the University of North Carolina at Charlotte and project codirector of the U.S. Department of Education–supported Behavior and Reading Improvement Center. With 25 years of research experience and extensive first-hand knowledge of teaching students classified as seriously emotionally disturbed (and other equally useless terms), Algozzine is a uniquely qualified staff developer, conference speaker, and teacher of behavior management and effective teaching courses.

As an active partner and collaborator with professionals in the Charlotte-Mecklenburg schools in North Carolina and as an editor of several journals focused on special education, Algozzine keeps his finger on the pulse of current special education practice. He has written more than 250 manuscripts on special education topics, authoring many popular books and textbooks on how to manage emotional and social behavior problems. Through *A Practical Approach to Special Education for Every Teacher,* Algozzine hopes to continue to help improve the lives of students with special needs—and the professionals who teach them.

Jim Ysseldyke, PhD, is Birkmaier Professor in the Department of Educational Psychology, director of the School Psychology Program, and director of the Center for Reading Research at the University of Minnesota. Widely requested as a staff developer and conference speaker, he brings more than 30 years of research and teaching experience to educational professionals around the globe.

As the former director of the federally funded National Center on Educational Outcomes, Ysseldyke conducted research and provided technical support that helped to boost the academic performance of students with disabilities and improve school assessment techniques nationally. Today he continues to work to improve the education of students with disabilities.

The author of more than 300 publications on special education and school psychology, Ysseldyke is best known for his textbooks on assessment, effective instruction, issues in special education, and other cutting-edge areas of education and school psychology. With *A Practical Approach to Special Education for Every Teacher,* he seeks to equip educators with practical knowledge and methods that will help them to better engage students in exploring—and meeting—all their potentials.

Self-Assessment 1

Before you begin this book, check your knowledge of the content being covered. Choose the best answer for each of the following questions.

1. Four characteristics of effective instruction are

    a. Planning instruction, teaching, modeling, evaluating

    b. Planning, managing instruction, delivering instruction, evaluating

    c. Modeling examples, delivering instruction, evaluating, revising

    d. Planning instruction, managing behavior, providing feedback, evaluating

2. _____ is the systematic presentation of content assumed necessary for mastery within a general area of knowledge.

    a. Coaching

    b. Presenting

    c. Evaluating

    d. Teaching

3. _____ means making decisions about what information to present, how to present the information, and how to communicate realistic expectations to students.

    a. Planning

    b. Setting goals

    c. Presenting

    d. Modeling

4. Which type of information is gathered by administering criterion-referenced tests?

    a. Knowledge of specific skills that a student should not learn

    b. Intelligence and/or achievement levels

    c. Relative knowledge and grade consistencies

    d. Specific skills or content that a students knows or does not know

5. Which type of information is gathered by administering norm-referenced tests?

    a. Knowledge of specific skills that a student should learn

    b. Intelligence and/or achievement levels

    c. Relative knowledge and grade consistencies

    d. Specific skills or content that a students knows or does not know

6. The process of breaking a complex academic task into its component parts is called _____.

    a. Task analysis

    b. Differentiated instruction

    c. Direct instruction

    d. Task differentiation

7. The educational placement in which a student spends most of the school day with other students who have disabilities and with at least one special education teacher is called a _____.

a. Self-contained class

b. Special day class

c. Special resource class

d. Special-special class

8. Teachers can make classroom environments positive by _____.

a. Having very strict and consistent rules

b. Using praise to support accomplishments

c. Teaching students to follow their own rules

d. Building strong relationships with other teachers

9. Evaluation that occurs at the end of instruction is called _____.

a. Cumulative evaluation

b. Terminal evaluation

c. Summative evaluation

d. Formative evaluation

10. Evaluation that occurs during instruction is called _____.

a. Cumulative evaluation

b. Terminal evaluation

c. Summative evaluation

d. Formative evaluation

REFLECTION

After you answer the multiple-choice questions, think about how you would answer the following questions:

- What do effective teachers do?
- What are some approaches that have been successful with students with disabilities?
- What is the difference between effective instruction in general and special education classrooms?

Introduction to Effective Instruction for Students With Special Needs

I **nstruction** is a general term that means providing knowledge in a systematic way. Teaching is one form of instruction and computer-assisted instruction is another. In computer-assisted instruction, a computer program serves as the primary method for providing knowledge. Traditionally, teaching has been the primary form of instruction (Algozzine, Ysseldyke, & Elliott, 1997; Entwistle, Skinner, Entwistle, & Orr, 2000; Ethell & McMeniman, 2000; Ho, 2000; Kember, Kwan, & Ledesma, 2001; Samuelowicz & Bain, 2001; Yost, Sentner, & Forlenza-Bailey, 2000). **Teaching** is the systematic presentation of content assumed necessary for mastery within a general area of knowledge. Teaching is most effective when certain principles are followed. According to Ornstein and Levine (1993, p. 617), teachers are most effective when they:

- Make sure that students know how they are expected to perform.
- Let students know how to obtain help.
- Follow through with reminders and rewards to enforce rules.
- Provide smooth transitions between activities.
- Give students assignments of sufficient variety to maintain interest.
- Monitor the class for signs of confusion or inattention.
- Use variations in eye contact, voice, and movement to maintain student attention.
- Use variations in academic activities to maintain student attention.
- Do not respond to discipline problems emotionally.
- Arrange the physical environment to complement instruction.

- Do not embarrass students in front of their classmates.
- Respond flexibly to unexpected developments.

These are just some of the ways in which effective teachers provide knowledge systematically. They are representative of the four components of effective instruction that frame the contents of this book.

1

What Are the Components of Effective Instruction?

Teaching is the systematic presentation of content assumed necessary for mastery within a general area of knowledge. **Instruction** is a general term that means providing knowledge in a systematic way. The characteristics of effective instruction can be represented in four groups:

1. Planning instruction

2. Managing instruction

3. Delivering instruction

4. Evaluating instruction

All teachers plan, manage, deliver, and evaluate their instruction, whether they are working with students who are gifted, students with disabilities, or students without special needs.

PLANNING INSTRUCTION

If all students in a class were at the same instructional level and if the goals and objectives of schooling were clearly prescribed and the same for all students, then instruction would consist of doing the same things with all students, in the right order, at the right time. But all students are not alike, and the goals and objectives of instruction are not the same for all students. This is why planning is such an important part of instruction.

Planning means making decisions—about what information to present, how to present the information, and how to communicate realistic expectations to students. Planning instruction, then, involves three steps:

1. Deciding what to teach

2. Deciding how to teach

3. Communicating realistic expectations

Each of these three steps for planning instruction includes specific tasks. Use *Table 1.1* as a quick reference to the steps and tasks that comprise effective instructional planning.

Table 1.1   First Component of Effective Instruction: **Planning**

Deciding What to Teach

1. Assessing students' skills
2. Analyzing the instructional task
3. Establishing a logical instructional sequence
4. Considering contextual variables
5. Analyzing instructional groupings
6. Identifying gaps between actual and expected performance

Deciding How to Teach

1. Setting instructional goals
2. Selecting instructional methods and materials
3. Pacing instruction appropriately
4. Monitoring performance and replanning instruction

Communicating Realistic Expectations

1. Actively involving students in learning
2. Explicitly stating expectations
3. Maintaining high standards

Deciding What to Teach

Deciding what to teach enables teachers to match instruction to each student's skill level. The process of deciding what to teach includes:

- Assessing students' skills
- Analyzing the instructional task
- Establishing a logical instructional sequence
- Considering contextual variables
- Analyzing instructional groupings
- Identifying gaps between actual and expected performance

Assessing Students' Skills

In making decisions about what to teach, educators have to assess their students' skill levels. They have to identify which skills students have and which skills they do not have. Typically, teachers assess students using tests, observations, and interviews. Much of this assessment goes on during instruction. For example, some teachers assess students' performance by asking them to read aloud from their books, spell the words on their spelling lists, or solve the problems that are in their math texts. Teachers use this kind of informal assessment along with the results of achievement tests to plan their instruction.

Achievement tests indicate students' level of knowledge in academic content areas (e.g., mathematics, reading, science, social studies). **Norm-referenced tests** are used to compare students to each other and to groups on which the test was originally developed. **Criterion-referenced tests** are used to compare students to standards of mastery relative to the content being measured. Using norm-referenced tests, teachers can make judgments about their students' knowledge relative to other students taking the test. They can also estimate the grade levels at which their students are performing. Using criterion-referenced tests, teachers can identify the specific skills their students have or have not mastered. With an understanding of students' academic and behavioral strengths and weaknesses, teachers can modify their instructional methods to meet the needs of individual students.

Analyzing the Instructional Task

It is not enough to know what students are able to do; teachers also must know exactly what it is they want students to do. Only then can they match content to their students' skill level. Part of deciding what to teach is analyzing the instructional task. **Task analysis** consists of breaking down a complex task into its component parts. For example, to solve the problem 105×3, a student must understand numerals, know the meaning of the multiplication sign, and have a basic understanding of both place value and multiplication. All of these components of the task must be taught to students before they will be able to solve the problem.

Establishing a Logical Instructional Sequence

Task analysis helps teachers plan a logical sequence of instruction. Students are more likely to learn if teachers present material in a clear, logical sequence. When planning what to teach, teachers must understand that the acquisition of new skills depends on the learning of lower-level skills.

Considering Contextual Variables

Contextual variables also play a part in deciding what to teach. Relevant **contextual variables** may include where instruction will take place, how long the lesson(s) will be, and who will be in the room during instruction. For example, knowing that a lesson requires the use of special materials (e.g., science equipment, computers, library resources) or more than the usual amount of instructional time is essential before starting the lesson.

Analyzing Instructional Groupings

In planning what to teach, effective teachers consider the instructional groupings that work best in their classrooms. Knowing that having one or two students working together at a computer is the most efficient use of the technology directs teachers as much as knowing that some students perform better in small groups or that a large group is the best way to present directions for an independent assignment. Usually teachers present material to students in groups, but sometimes they teach students individually. It is important to consider your students' performances, behaviors, and skills when they are in particular instructional groupings, as well as the physical space and the ways in which students interact in it.

Identifying Gaps in Actual and Expected Performance

In deciding what to teach, teachers must identify any gaps that exist between a student's actual level of performance and the expected level of performance. By recognizing the difference between actual performance and expected performance, teachers are able to keep instructional goals and objectives realistic, neither too low nor too high.

Deciding How to Teach

It is difficult to know ahead of time how best to teach. Teaching is an experimental process: Effective teachers try approaches and materials until they find the combination that works best in moving students toward instructional objectives. You may have thought, or even been told in courses, that the way to decide how to teach a student is to give a battery of tests, identify the student's strengths and weaknesses, then remediate weaknesses or build up strengths. But this is not enough. Yes, it is important to take into account a student's level of skill and to identify learning and behavioral strengths and weaknesses, but simply knowing a student's score on a test cannot help you decide how to teach the student.

In making decisions about how to teach, teachers must make an educated guess about the kinds of approaches that will work, then try those approaches and monitor the results. That educated guess is based on experience, either with a particular student or with others like that student. After that, the only way to decide how to teach is to teach, then to gather data to determine its effectiveness. This does not mean that you should teach blindly. Experience provides a basic understanding of what works and what does not work. Also, check the literature for guidelines of effective instruction like these (Wittrock, 1986):

- Begin with an overview or use advance organizers and lists of objectives to set the stage for a presentation.
- Signal transitions between parts of a lesson and review or summarize subparts as the lesson proceeds.
- Ask questions of varying levels of difficulty throughout a presentation.
- Control the pace and continuity of lessons by regulating the time allowed for students to ask or answer questions.

In addition to making an educated guess and consulting the literature, four activities come into play when you are deciding how to teach:

- Setting instructional goals
- Selecting instructional methods and materials
- Pacing instruction appropriately
- Monitoring performance and replanning instruction

Setting Instructional Goals

The process of deciding how to teach begins with setting instructional goals for individual students, then establishing an instructional sequence. Most complex skills consist of combinations of simpler or lower-level skills. These lower-level skills must be taught in a logical sequence in order for students to acquire the complex skill.

Selecting Instructional Methods and Materials

The next step in deciding how to teach is to choose appropriate methods and materials. This relatively easy task can become complicated when students have special needs. Students may require alternative methods (e.g., sign language or acceleration) or may need special instructional materials (e.g., tape-recorded lessons, advanced reading materials, high interest/low-level vocabulary reading books). Together, alternative methods and materials can be a powerful teaching combination. For example, students with learning disabilities may be reading Shakespeare's *Macbeth* in the general education classroom and, in addition, may be using an alternative form of the play in their special education classrooms, testing their comprehension with verbal quizzes and discussions after each scene of the play.

Pacing Instruction Appropriately

Setting a pace is also part of the process of figuring out how to teach. **Pace** is how quickly or slowly the class moves through the material. In addition to pace, teachers need to set a ratio of known to unknown material and set standard rates of success. Effective instruction includes about 75 percent known and 25 percent unknown material. Students should be expected to demonstrate about 80 percent mastery with this combination.

Monitoring Performance and Replanning Instruction

Probably the most important part of deciding how to teach is monitoring student performance and then using that information to plan subsequent instruction. Deciding *what* to teach is a form of diagnosis; deciding *how* to teach is a prescription, a treatment. If that treatment is not appropriate to the individual's needs, it can lead to educational problems.

Communicating Realistic Expectations

The third component of instructional planning is setting realistic expectations for students and communicating those expectations to them. When teachers do not expect much from their students, they are shortchanging them. If they have the skills to do so, students will, over time, learn to perform at the level of expectation that teachers hold for them (Good & Brophy, 1984). When those expectations are realistically high, students succeed; when they are unrealistically low, students fail.

Actively Involving Students in Learning

To communicate realistic expectations, teachers first have to get students active and involved in learning. Students who do not take part in learning activities cannot be expected to demonstrate high levels of performance on classroom quizzes and tests. This is particularly important when students have disabilities.

Explicitly Stating Expectations

Communicating realistic expectations is a process of telling students (and being sure they understand) what it is they are expected to learn and what they have to do to learn it. It is also important to help students understand the consequences of failure and how to turn mistakes into opportunities for new learning.

Maintaining High Standards

Too often, teachers decide that students with special needs cannot handle the same assignments as other students, and so they set separate standards for those students. Unanimously, students with disabilities and parents of students with disabilities in every educational setting complain that adapting or accommodating to disability all too often results in lowered expectations and patronization. They contend that disability sometimes requires modification and adaptation but never patronization. Accommodating without patronizing requires students, their families, fellow classmates, and professionals to adopt a standard of inclusion in activities and an expectation of meeting norms of performance set for an activity (Asch, 1989).

MANAGING INSTRUCTION

Managing instruction includes preparing for instruction, using time productively, and creating a positive environment. *Table 1.2* outlines the steps and tasks of managing instruction.

Table 1.2 Second Component of Effective Instruction: **Managing Instruction**

Preparing for Instruction

- Setting and communicating classroom rules
- Teaching consequences of behavior
- Handling disruptions efficiently
- Teaching students self-management

Using Time Productively

- Establishing routines and procedures
- Organizing the physical space
- Keeping transitions brief
- Limiting interruptions
- Using an academic, task-oriented focus
- Allocating sufficient time to academics

Creating a Positive Environment

- Making the classroom a friendly place
- Accepting individual differences
- Keeping interactions positive
- Involving students

Preparing for Instruction

Few of us are comfortable in chaos. We need order around us. Students, too, need an orderly environment in which to learn. They need rules to follow; they need an understanding of those rules and to know what the consequences will be if they do not follow them; and they need to see that the rules are enforced. In addition to rule-setting, preparing for instruction includes deciding how you will react to disruptions and how you will teach students to manage their own behavior. In order to manage instruction effectively, you must establish and communicate rules for behavior in the classroom early in the school year. Students need to understand the importance of following rules and the consequences of not following them. When disruptions occur, teachers must handle them quickly, as soon as possible after they happen, and consistently. Prompt, consistent action helps the class settle back down and refocus its attention on the work at hand.

One factor that limits the integration of students with disabilities into general education settings is that teachers can become overwhelmed with managing problem behaviors. One solution is to teach students to manage their own behavior. There are several self-management procedures that are easy to use. One procedure is to place an index card on some of the students' desks. At the top of each card, write a question that is appropriate for the student. One student may have the question "Am I paying attention?" Another student may have the question "Did I raise my hand?" With the index cards in place, teach students to periodically check their own behavior and record their performance by making a mark on their cards if they are doing what they are supposed to be doing. Check the cards during the day and give students feedback on their self-monitoring and behavior.

Using Time Productively

The second principle of managing instruction is using time productively. Teachers must teach; they must present academic content and other instructional material. But they also must manage learning environments so that students are able to learn (e.g., they organize the classroom so time is not wasted finding materials or moving between activities). What does a well-managed instructional environment look like?

- Time is used productively.
- Transitions between activities are brief.
- Few interruptions break the flow of classroom activities.
- The classroom has an active, task-oriented focus.
- Sufficient time is allocated to academic activities.

Creating a Positive Environment

Students are more motivated to learn when teachers accept their individual differences, interact positively with them, and create a supportive, cooperative classroom atmosphere. Students feel better about school and about learning when their teachers demonstrate acceptance and caring.

DELIVERING INSTRUCTION

Many people go into teaching because they want to share what they know and help others be successful. Teachers enjoy sharing their knowledge using appropriate instructional principles. The third component of effective instruction, delivering instruction, is a three-stage process that involves:

- Presenting content
- Monitoring student learning
- Adjusting instruction

The tasks associated with these three stages are outlined in *Tables 1.3a* and *1.3b*.

Presenting Content

Table 1.3a outlines the tasks associated with the first stage of delivering instruction: presenting content. Effective teachers present well-crafted lessons. They also teach thinking skills so their students can apply what they are learning rather than just repeat back memorized facts. In addition, effective teachers are responsible for motivating students, so they provide varied opportunities for their students to practice what they are learning.

Presenting Lessons

The first thing teachers must do when they present lessons is to obtain their students' attention. Students cannot learn unless they are attentive and involved in the instructional process. Effective instruction begins with a review of previously taught

Table 1.3a Third Component of Effective Instruction: **Delivering Instruction**

Presenting Content

- Presenting Lessons
- Making lessons relevant
- Maintaining student attention
- Communicating the goals of instruction
- Checking student understanding

Teaching Thinking Skills

- Modeling thinking skills
- Teaching learning strategies

Motivating Students

- Showing enthusiasm
- Assigning work that reflects students' interests
- Using rewards intermittently
- Assigning work at which students can succeed

Providing Relevant Practice

- Teaching skills to mastery
- Varying the instructional materials

skills or content. New content is best introduced within the context of material with which students are familiar. Skills necessary to complete a new lesson need to be reviewed and reinforced.

Teachers should also make lessons relevant to individual students. To do this, teachers have to be knowledgeable about their students and the social environment in which their students live. Students in rural North Dakota have different frames of reference than students in inner-city classrooms. It makes sense, then, to use different examples when teaching them. Lessons that are relevant help to maintain students' attention. Other ways to gain and keep students' attention are to be enthusiastic, to be organized, and to pace instruction. It's also important to interact positively with students, be supportive of their efforts, and help them avoid negative comments, put-downs, and criticism.

Another essential ingredient of an effective presentation is an early statement of instructional goals. Clear communication of instructional demands and intent sets the stage for success. Written and oral directions need to be easy to understand, complete, and in logical order. It's important to check that students understand the material you are teaching. The best way to do this is to check their understanding before they start to practice a new skill. This prevents students from practicing incorrectly. It is also important to check that students understand what they are supposed to do. Many teachers do this by having students go through the steps they will use to solve a problem before they actually do the work. We recently watched this process in a math lesson. Ms. Crews, a special education teacher in Gainesville, Florida, asked her students to describe how they would solve the assigned two-digit addition problems before they started to work on them. Each student described the process he or she would use. Some said they would start at the upper left-hand corner and work across the first line; others said they would start in different places. Ms. Crews told them she did not mind where they started as long as they did each problem by adding the right column together before going to the left. She also carefully monitored what the students said they would do when the sum of the first column was greater than nine.

Teaching Thinking Skills

The second part of presenting content is teaching thinking skills. Students need to be taught more than how to do something by rote memory. Most studies of effective instruction contend that by teaching thinking skills, teachers enhance the quality of their lessons. There are a couple of ways to teach thinking skills. First, teachers can *model thinking skills;* that is, they can show students how to do what they expect them to do. Second, teachers can directly *teach learning strategies,* explaining how and why students' responses are right or wrong and explaining the processes that must be used to complete the task.

Motivating Students

Motivating students is the third part of presenting content. Effective teachers know the importance of motivating students. They know that students learn better when they are motivated. How do you motivate students? First, you have to show enthusiasm and interest in the material you present. Second, you have to get students to understand the importance of assigned tasks. One way to do this is to design work that reflects individual students' interests and experiences. Rewards can motivate students, but they should be used sparingly. Students who are constantly rewarded for what they do soon lose interest. Instead, rewards should be administered intermittently to maintain attention and behavior.

Another strategy to motivate students is to make them believe they can do the work. Two simple methods work here: (a) maintaining a warm, supportive atmosphere and (b) selecting and using instructional activities at which you know students can succeed.

Providing Relevant Practice

Providing relevant practice is an important part of presenting content. Students master material when they have opportunities to practice. Whether they practice under a teacher's direction or independently, it is important that the tasks they work on and the materials they work with be relevant to achieving instructional goals. Students also need ample time to practice skills independently.

Teaching skills that students can master 90 percent to 100 percent of the time is essential. With relevant practice over adequate time periods, and with high levels of success, students develop **automaticity**; that is, they complete tasks and demonstrate skills automatically. Having students engage in extensive relevant practice is important, but if instructional materials are not varied, then practice becomes boring and interferes with instructional goals.

Monitoring Student Learning

The second aspect of delivering instruction is monitoring students' learning. Monitoring includes providing feedback, encouraging students, class discussions, working one on one with students, and more. The tasks associated with monitoring student learning are outlined in *Table 1.3b* along with those for adjusting instruction.

Feedback, providing information about a student's performance, is an essential part of monitoring learning. Effective teachers give students immediate, frequent, explicit feedback on their performance or behavior. When students do something correctly, they should be told so. When they do something incorrectly, they should be corrected. It is important to use praise and encouragement, tying them to a specific task. "I like the way you used your number line to add your numbers correctly" tells the student what he or she did right; diffuse praise (e.g., "Nice work!") leaves the student wondering. One way to provide corrective feedback is to explain the material again. Especially for students with learning difficulties, it is often necessary to explain many times how to accomplish a specific task. Teachers can also model correct performance. It is often necessary, and helpful, to show students specifically how to complete academic tasks.

Students should be actively responding to instruction. One way to involve students is to use their names during

Table 1.3b   Third Component of Effective Instruction:
            Delivering Instruction

Monitoring Student Learning

- Giving feedback
- Actively involving students
- Redirecting students who are off-task
- Providing ways for students to request help

Adjusting Instruction

- Varying instructional approaches
- Varying materials
- Adjusting pace

instructional sessions and move around the room. Another way to involve students is to teach them to be active learners. In well-managed classrooms, teachers use strategies that increase the time students spend on tasks. This is an important part of monitoring instruction. Teachers should keep an eye out for students who are not busy and redirect them. This can be done by visually scanning the room or by walking around the room and checking students' work. Work individually with any students who finish tasks early. Don't let students spend a lot of time waiting for the next part of the lesson. It's important to establish mechanisms for students to get needed help. Students who need help can be asked to sit quietly at their desks with a hand raised until you are able to help them. Or they can be asked to move to a special workstation, where help is provided by a paraprofessional or a peer.

Adjusting Instruction

The tasks associated with adjusting instruction, the third component of delivering instruction, are outlined in *Table 1.3b*. Adjusting instruction includes varying approaches for presenting content. All students do not learn in the same way or at the same pace. Teachers have to adjust their instruction for individual learners. There are no specific rules about how to modify lessons to meet all students' needs. The process usually is one of trial and error. Teachers try alternative approaches until one works. An example: Mr. Cruise was teaching a lesson on the characteristics of dinosaurs. During the lesson, he noticed that Tim was not paying attention. Another student, Susan, asked to go to the bathroom, and a third student started drumming on his desk with two pencils. It was clear to Mr. Cruise that the students were not interested in the lesson, so he modified it, assigning to each dinosaur the name of one of the students. He saved the most powerful, Tyrannosaurus Rex, for the end of the lesson and named him "Mr. Cruise." He believed this slight change was enough to interest the students in the lesson, and he was right.

Teachers can also adjust instruction by varying their methods and materials. This increases the chances of meeting individual students' needs. For students who are having difficulty, teachers can provide extra instruction and review or they can adjust the pace of instruction.

EVALUATING INSTRUCTION

Evaluation is the process by which teachers decide whether the methods and materials they are using are effective—based on students' performance. There are two kinds of evaluation: formative and summative. Both involve data collection. **Formative evaluation** occurs during the process of instruction. The teacher collects data during instruction and uses the data to make instructional decisions. **Summative evaluation** occurs at the end of instruction, when the teacher administers a test to determine whether the students have met instructional objectives. There are six components in the evaluation process:

- Monitoring students' understanding
- Monitoring engaged time
- Maintaining records of students' progress
- Informing students about their progress
- Using data to make decisions
- Making judgments about students' performance

The evaluation process is outlined in *Table 1.4* and described in the sections that follow.

Monitoring Student Understanding

Students need to know what teachers expect them to do, which means teachers must monitor the extent to which students understand directions. This involves more than asking a student, "Do you understand what you are supposed to do?" It's too easy for students to say "yup" without having the foggiest idea of what's expected. Instead, ask students to tell you or show you what they are going to do.

Students must also understand the process they need to go through to complete their assignments. You can check their

Table 1.4   Fourth Component of Effective Instruction:
Evaluating Instruction

Monitoring Student Understanding

- Monitoring student understanding of directions
- Monitoring the processes students use to do their work
- Checking success rates

Monitoring Engaged Time

- Ensuring active engagement
- Self-monitoring of participation
- Scanning for engagement

Maintaining Records of Student Progress

- Maintaining records
- Self-charting progress

Informing Students of Progress

- Informing students regularly
- Providing feedback
- Correcting errors
- Providing task-specific praise
- Self-correcting

Using Data to Make Decisions

- Deciding when to refer
- Making teaching changes
- Deciding when to discontinue service

Making Judgments About Student Performance

- Specifying goals for students
- Charting progress with aim lines

understanding by either asking them to show you what they are going to do or asking them to describe the process of responding to questions or solving problems.

One method you can use to monitor students' understanding is simply to check their success rate. Think about it for a moment. If you were to show a student how to solve double-digit addition problems, send her off to solve a page of 20 problems, and find out that she got 8 of the 20 correct, what would you conclude? You probably would conclude that she did not have a good understanding of the task. If, on the other hand, she got 19 of 20 correct, you could assume that she did understand the process. Data on student success rates tell us a great deal about the extent to which they understand what we ask them to do.

Monitoring Engaged Time

Students who answer direct questions and participate in discussions during instruction learn more in school. Teachers monitor the amount of time their students are actively involved in lessons by noting the extent to which they are participating in classroom activities. For example, Ms. Kleinman wanted to know whether one of her students was actively participating in the class discussion on various types of trees. As an index of involvement and participation, she kept track of the number of times the student raised his hand and the number of times he asked questions.

Keeping track of students' participation can be a time-consuming task. One way to make it easier is to teach students to monitor their own participation. You can keep a chart in your room that lists each student's name. At the end of every class, have students record the number of times they asked a question during the lesson. You can also have them place a plus sign, minus sign, or equal sign after the number to indicate if they did better (+), worse (–), or about the same (=) as the day before. At the end of the week, have them evaluate their overall performance and write a note to take home describing how they did in class during the week.

Effective teachers also gather data on student engagement by scanning the classroom to see who is actively involved in instruction. Periodically, teachers record the results of these observations and award free time or other prizes to students who meet criteria they have set for expected levels of involvement.

Maintaining Records of Student Progress

To know the extent to which students are profiting from instruction, teachers must keep records of their progress. Record-keeping can be informal or formal. Some teachers keep relatively informal records of students' progress in math, simply writing down the number of problems completed and the number or percentage completed correctly.

In other subjects, teachers may keep more formal records, such as charts of the number of words read correctly. *Figure 1.1* is a graph of a student's reading performance. Along the bottom of the chart are the number of days being evaluated. Along the left side are the numbers of words read correctly. Each day a point is made on the chart for the number of words read correctly that day. Then the points are connected to form a line that shows the student's progress reading words correctly. Both the student's performance and the goal can be indicated on the chart. The chart can then be used as a visual aid in making decisions about the student's rate of progress toward meeting specific objectives.

Charting, like monitoring engaged time, can be a lot of work, particularly in a large class. Here, too, students can learn to keep

Figure 1.1 Bobby's Reading Performance

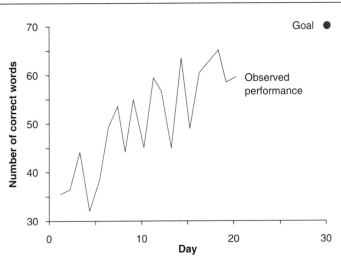

track of their own performance. For instance, you may teach students how to chart the percentage of math problems that they solved correctly each day. This frees up your time, but, more importantly, it keeps students actively involved in their own learning and gives them a sense of accomplishment.

Informing Students of Progress

By providing regular feedback you can keep students informed about their progress. That way they know what is expected of them and the extent to which they are meeting expectations. Feedback should be frequent and quick. Students are more apt to learn material when they know how they are performing and when their errors are corrected quickly, before mistakes become habits.

Task-specific praise is most effective. It's not enough to simply tell Manuel that he did a good job; we have to tell him what we mean when we say "Good job." For example: "Manuel, you did a very nice job of filling in the names of the countries on your map; you got them all correct."

When students make mistakes, it's good practice to have them correct their mistakes immediately. Effective teachers make sure that students do not practice errors. One student teacher had her class complete a math worksheet while she worked individually with a student who was having trouble. She didn't pay much attention to the other students because they were quiet and busy. She assumed the activity was instructionally appropriate. Later, when she reviewed the other students' work, she found that one student had done all the problems on the sheet using the wrong algorithm. She realized that she should have monitored the student's work.

Using Data to Make Decisions

Records are important, not only for charting students' progress, but also for making decisions about students' educational programs. For example, suppose the child-study team is considering placing a student in a **self-contained class** (one in which the student spends most of the school day with other students who have disabilities and with at least one special education teacher). Before they make that decision, members of the team want to know what has been done instructionally with the student in the general education classroom and the extent to which he or she has profited from instruction there. If the teacher has kept proper records or, better yet, charted the student's progress, the data are readily accessible.

The decision to discontinue special education services also rests on information about the student's progress and that of his or her agemates. When teachers keep track of an individual student's progress, and know the progress of the rest of the class, they can make **normative peer comparisons** (judgments about the performance of the individual student relative to the average performance of his or her peers).

Direct, frequent data on student performance can also be used to make instructional decisions. By keeping track of students' progress, teachers can decide whether the approach or materials they are using are effective. Although monitoring a student's progress does not tell a teacher how to teach that student, it does tell the teacher the extent to which the student is making the kind of progress expected.

Making Judgments About Student Performance

By regularly measuring students' performance, teachers are able to make judgments. To measure progress, teachers must specify their goals for individual students and then plot an aim line. An **aim line** shows the rate of ongoing progress that is necessary for a student to achieve a particular goal. In *Figure 1.2*, the aim line is the straight line. This is the rate of progress necessary to meet the instructional goal. The student's progress (the dotted line) is then charted in comparison to the aim line.

Figure 1.2 Courtney's Reading Progress

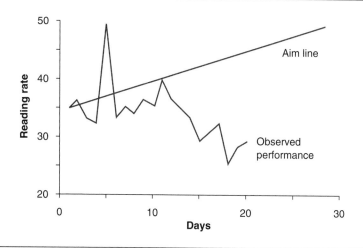

Note that the teacher still has to make a critical judgment about the goal. Does the teacher want or expect the student to achieve the same instructional goals that are held for all students in the school? Or does the teacher want the student to achieve goals that are more specific?

2

What Methods Should Teachers Use to Teach Students Who Are Exceptional?

More than ever before, general and special education teachers are working together to accommodate students with special learning needs, and students with learning needs are being taught in classroom environments that are as much like general education classrooms as possible. Through combinations of individualized instruction, small- and large-group instruction, and teacher- and student-directed instruction, teachers are adapting learning experiences for all students.

Wang (1989) describes several ways teachers adapt instruction for students with special needs:

Instruction is based on the assessed capabilities of each student.

Teachers provide varying amounts of instruction and use a variety of approaches to work with students individually or in groups.

Materials and procedures permit each student to progress in the mastery of instructional content at a pace suited to his or her abilities and interests.

Periodic and systematic evaluations of student progress serve to inform individual students of their mastery of academic skills and content.

Each student undertakes, with teacher assistance and coaching, increasing responsibility for identifying his or her learning needs, as well as the resources required to perform tasks, plan learning activities, and evaluate mastery.

Alternate activities and materials are available to aid students in the acquisition of essential academic skills and content.

Students have opportunities to make choices and decisions about their individual learning goals, their specific learning activities, and consequently, their own learning outcomes.

Students assist each other in pursuing individual goals, and they cooperate in achieving group goals. (p. 102)

The principles of adapting instruction (as suggested by Wang, 1989) are no different from the principles of instruction that have been shown to be effective with all students. You may be asking yourself if there are any special teaching methods for students who are exceptional. If you watched general and special education teachers working with students who are exceptional, you would notice many similarities in the ways they teach. You would probably also notice some differences.

(Text continues on page 37)

Window on Practice

My name is Karen Richards, and I was a student intern from the University of Florida assigned to a public school for students with mental retardation in Gainesville, Florida. For 11 weeks I taught social skills, reading, and math, and assumed all of the responsibilities of my supervising teacher, with the exception of collecting the paycheck.

Student Teaching: The Final Exam

I was finally ready to put those hours of lectures, notes, theories, lesson plans, and materials to the test. It's common to start doubting yourself and begin asking yourself things like, "Do I really know enough about teaching to take over a whole class? Did I need to learn all that stuff? Do I really want to be a special educator?" Soon you realize that everyone else is asking themselves the same questions and you feel relieved.

Your student teaching experience begins with paperwork—lots of paperwork. The application I had to fill out looked like a novel. It included three copies each of a biographical sketch, resume, picture, letters of reference, career center registration cards, and the classic essay, "Why do you want to be a teacher?" You ought to pass your student teaching internship just for being able to fill out your application correctly! Could this really be preparing you for the field of special education?

The next step is waiting. You hope and pray that you won't be assigned to a "bad" school or to a "slave driver" teacher. It is usually close to the month before your internship is to begin that you receive your assignment. I found that visiting the classroom before I began teaching was a big help. It gave me a chance to meet my supervising teacher and aide, to see the class in action, and best of all, it gave the kids a chance to meet me and get accustomed to my being in the classroom. Because of these early visits, I felt very comfortable around all these people. When my internship began, I was able to jump right into action.

The real test of your ability comes when you take over the classroom, usually in the third or fourth week of your internship. You become the planner, the decision-maker, the clock watcher, the audio-visual genius, the cheerleader, and whatever else it takes to fill your supervising teacher's shoes. You discover that nobody has the time to write the kind of lesson plans you learned to write in college. You discover that adequate classroom materials are nonexistent. You discover that parents are not always cooperative. You discover that paperwork takes up a lot of good teaching time. You discover that a lot of teachers are getting by with minimum effort. And, after all this discovering, you realize that college has prepared you to teach the ideal class in the

(Continued)

(Continued)

ideal classroom, one that you seldom, if ever, get assigned to as an intern. Welcome to the real world. You will learn, you will make mistakes, and you will learn more. Once you accept this fact, you can start to enjoy yourself.

The success of your internship will be strongly influenced by your supervising teacher. He or she can be an invaluable resource or a threatening observer, depending on how you wish to view the situation. Your specific responsibilities will vary depending on your teacher. After taking over my supervising teacher's responsibilities, I realized how much more there is to teaching than just teaching. I can honestly say I spent more time performing nonteaching duties than actually teaching. I happened to have a teacher who was extremely active in the school's projects and in outside activities involving her students, and I was expected to become involved in these same activities. Although interns are not required to go beyond school responsibilities, I feel that my involvement in outside activities greatly improved my relationship with my supervising teacher. I never felt intimidated or threatened by her, and she became an excellent role model. I didn't always agree with her ideas, but this made me realize how I would do things differently in my own classroom. An important thing to remember is that an intern is only temporary, and as much as you would like to, you can't make drastic changes in a classroom in 11 weeks. It will only frustrate your teacher, your students, and yourself.

Every internship experience is different. Having a roommate and many friends who were also student teaching made it impossible for me not to compare. We would talk about our experiences and realize that some of us had to do much more planning, while others had to spend much more time with extracurricular activities, and some seemed to have it much too easy. But one thing we all had in common was that we loved the kids. After all, that's why we chose this profession.

Probably the most useful statement I ever heard in college was, "Be a teacher to your students, not a buddy."

I found this out the hard way. You want so much for your students to like you that it becomes very hard to enforce your rules. Enjoy your kids, but remember why you are there.

At the end of 11 weeks I hated to leave. Fortunately, I had been applying for jobs while interning and landed a position before graduation. I now teach a class of students with emotional disabilities in an elementary school. My internship experience has greatly enhanced my ability to teach. Oh, there are still days when I ask myself, "Do I really want to be a special educator?" But then there are many more days when I wouldn't trade my job for anything.

—Karen Richards, a teacher of emotionally handicapped students in Virginia Beach, Virginia.

Window on Practice

As a resource room teacher, I work with high school students who have learning disabilities. The majority of students in my class come from very poor economic environments. Many have no parental support, and they haven't been taught social and moral ethics. Their academic needs often come second to their social needs. Along with meeting the academic and vocational needs of my students, I spend a great deal of time addressing their social needs and counseling them.

I teach my students to think for themselves, believe in themselves, and always be in tune with themselves. Throughout the year we take class time and have heart-to-heart talks about whatever they want to discuss. Some of the topics we've addressed this year include drugs, sex, the service, college, abuse, peer pressure, and cheating. My students call me "the preacher" because they say I preach to them about everyday things of life that no one has sat down and discussed with them before. I don't mind the

(Continued)

(Continued)

name—I think it's quite fitting. One of my students last year told me that I was the first teacher to care about him as a person, not just as a student.

The only difference I see between my job and that of a general education classroom teacher is I sometimes spend more time counseling than teaching because my students' social needs are so great. Don't get the idea that I skimp on covering the academic competencies I'm required to teach! I spend a great deal of time preparing my students so that they can do as well in their mainstreamed classes as in their resource room classes. But a lot of times I think educators overlook the social needs of students. If I need to address them during class time, then I'll do that because in the long run I know that my counseling is going to be just as helpful to them as my teaching. The way I see it, a child can't be taught new tricks until he or she understands the old tricks—or, another way of putting it, a child can't understand where he's going until he understands where he comes from.

Some of the major concerns I have about educating exceptional students center on their teachers' willingness to listen to them and to help them make their own decisions. Many exceptional students are not informed about postsecondary opportunities, and those who are often get the information too late. They may find out that they can go to college and receive financial aid, but if this information is not available to them until late in their secondary education, there may not be enough time for them to prepare for a college program right after graduation. Teachers need to ensure that students are adequately informed about opportunities. Teachers need to listen more carefully to exceptional students expressing their career preferences and to work with them in selecting a course of study that will help them reach their goals.

Anthony Wolfe is one student who has helped me learn a lot this year. He has helped me understand that even I need to work on listening to students more. At the beginning of the past school year, Anthony wanted to take an Algebra I course and I talked him out of it, saying, "No, you go ahead and take the Competency Math course." Halfway through the year I started to think that I hadn't made the best choice for Anthony. At the end of the year I knew I'd made a mistake. Anthony was talking about going to college and he had discovered that math requirements for college include Algebra I, Algebra II, and Geometry.

Anthony will have to attend summer school to pick up the math he needs for college. I limited Anthony by not listening to what he was trying to tell me. I realize that my students and I can learn a lot from each other. I usually tell them this at the outset of the school year because I want them to feel comfortable with me. I want to be of help to them in any way they need.

Students with learning disabilities can lead successful lives—they can go on to college if that is what they want to do. One of my primary goals as a teacher of exceptional students is to help them realize that it is okay to have a learning disability and to have to learn information differently. I hope they will learn to see that this disability does not have to control them, that they can use strategies to help them control it.

—Mabel Hines, a resource room teacher of students with learning disabilities at Terry Sanford Senior High School, Fayetteville, North Carolina.

There is a diversity of approaches used to meet the special learning needs of exceptional students in general education and special education classrooms. But there is no magic in these methods. They are simply used more often when students need help to learn. These methods include (Ysseldyke & Algozzine, 1990):

Behavior therapy

Precision teaching

Ability training

Direct instruction

Cognitive behavior modification

Cognitive skills training

Critical thinking

Counseling therapy

Learning strategies

Cooperative learning

Peer-directed learning

Peer tutoring

Classwide peer tutoring

Social skills training

Behavior Therapy

Behavior therapy is the process of systematically arranging environmental events to influence behavior. It assumes that stimuli and consequences can be used to increase, decrease, or maintain behaviors. And it is commonly used in working with students who have special needs.

Behavior therapy is based on the principles of respondent and operant conditioning. **Respondent conditioning** ties a reflex response to a new stimulus. Innate responses (reflexes) follow specific eliciting stimuli. For example, blowing air into your eyes causes you to blink. The frequency of the response is directly related to the frequency of the eliciting stimulus.

New stimuli can come to elicit innate responses through the process of conditioning. By continually pairing a stimulus that elicits a response with a new stimulus that does not normally elicit the response, the new stimulus comes to elicit the response when presented alone.

Operant conditioning is the systematic application and removal of rewards and punishments to increase wanted behaviors and to reduce unwanted behaviors. Behavior therapy approaches based on operant conditioning typically follow five steps:

1. Specifying a target behavior and a plan for measuring it

2. Identifying levels of the behavior before intervention

3. Selecting reinforcers (rewards or punishments) and formulating a plan for systematically applying them

4. Implementing the plan

5. Evaluating the effects of the intervention

PRECISION TEACHING

Precision teaching is one way teachers plan, use, and analyze the effects of their instructional methods on students' performance. The approach involves continuous evaluation of students' progress toward meeting instructional objectives and always focuses on improving skills. It is a five-step process:

1. The teacher pinpoints the target behavior.

2. The teacher or student counts and records the baseline rate of the behavior, a measure of performance before teaching begins.

3. Using this baseline information, the teacher writes a short-term objective.

4. The teacher tries an instructional method, recording and evaluating changes in the student's behavior.

5. If the evaluation indicates that the student's performance is inadequate, the teacher changes the instructional method.

Teachers who use precision teaching usually record each student's progress on a special record called a **standard behavior chart**, but some teachers just use graph paper to keep track of changes in behavior.

ABILITY TRAINING

Ability training means practicing skills presumed to underlie academic success (e.g., visually tracking from left to right) as a means of improving basic skill (e.g., reading) performance. When students need instruction in preacademic skills (e.g., differentiating visual stimuli and remembering them), their teachers use ability training to organize their special education experiences. For example, if a student has a problem seeing the differences among geometric shapes, letters, or numbers, the teacher might assign worksheets that require matching a figure with one like it. If a student has a problem differentiating the *sh* and *th* consonant blends or the vowel sounds of *a* and *e*, the teacher might assign tape-recorded activities to give the student practice. Often ability training involves practice in an area where a student has difficulty, but it is also an effective way to teach students to use their own strengths to compensate for deficits. For example, a child with poor auditory discrimination could be taught using a sight-word approach.

DIRECT INSTRUCTION

A teacher's actions are directly and functionally related to the goals of instruction. If a student has not mastered math skills involving division, an effective teacher arranges teaching activities to provide systematic, guided instruction in division facts. This approach is called **direct instruction**, and it relies on task analysis to identify the component steps of the skill that needs teaching.

Attack strategy training is a form of direct instruction in which students are taught the steps of a skill and rules for putting the steps together. Using attack strategy, students can solve problems that are alike (Lloyd, 1980). For example, in solving a multiplication problem like 2×4, students might be taught to read the problem and say, "Count by two, four times ("2, 4, 6, 8"), then say the last number in the sequence as the solution to the problem." Once learned, the same strategy can be used to attack similar problems (3×4, 4×2, and so on). Attack strategy training works like this:

Analyze the curriculum content to determine the skills to be taught.

Devise a strategy for attacking problems that require the application of the skill.

Analyze the attack strategy to decide how to teach it.

Teach the attack strategy and evaluate performance.

In addition to task analysis, direct instruction utilizes modeling of expected behavior, corrective and supportive feedback, and independent practice.

COGNITIVE BEHAVIOR MODIFICATION

Cognitive behavior modification teaches students to use self-statements to improve their performance on academic and other skills. For example, some teachers have taught students to evaluate whether they are paying attention by having them use a checklist taped to their desks, like the one in *Figure 2.1.* Each student has a personal question (Am I paying attention? Am I doing what I'm supposed to be doing?) at the top of the checklist and a place to make marks to represent affirmative answers to the question. Research shows that students who have been taught to evaluate their performance by "talking to themselves" this way have improved their performance in academic skill areas.

COGNITIVE SKILLS TRAINING

Many teachers believe that students should be taught thinking skills as part of their schooling. The most widely recognized grouping (taxonomy) of educational objectives in the cognitive domain was developed by Benjamin Bloom (1956). Bloom's taxonomy identifies six levels of cognitive skills—knowledge, comprehension, application, analysis, synthesis, and evaluation—each more complex than the one before it (Clark, 1983).

Knowledge

To teach knowledge skills, teachers expose students to aesthetic, economic, political, educational, and social aspects of the environment and to people with similar interests. Teachers then have students conduct **needs assessments** (determining the necessary information or principles for successful completion of the project) and organize their data.

Comprehension and Application

Comprehension and application skills include collecting information to use in decision making, working with

Figure 2.1   Checklist

Name _____

Week of _____

Am I Paying Attention?

Monday	
Tuesday	
Wednesday	
Thursday	
Friday	

people who share common interests, and developing original products.

Analysis and Synthesis

Analysis and synthesis skills include examining creative products, changing ways of thinking, comparing thinking patterns with others, and integrating knowledge using convergent and divergent thinking strategies.

Evaluation

Identifying standards for making comparisons, developing decision-making skills, and making choices are all evaluation skills.

CRITICAL THINKING

Teaching students to think should be a goal of all teachers. Critical-thinking objectives are central to the instruction of students with special needs because thinking skills have enormous potential to improve students' lives.

COUNSELING THERAPY

Teachers and related-services professionals may focus on students' interpersonal skills. Many teachers structure classroom activities to accommodate the social and emotional problems of their students. This is a form of **counseling therapy** (using interpersonal conversations and carefully structured experiences to influence behaviors).

A number of practices are used in this approach. For example, in **reality therapy**, the teacher helps students identify the problem and ways to rectify it (Glaser, 1965). In **client-centered therapy**, the teacher creates a warm, permissive environment that encourages students to express themselves and to develop their own problem-solving strategies (C. Rogers, 1951). In this kind of interaction, the teacher avoids making evaluative statements of any type.

In **transactional analysis (TA)**, teachers identify communication patterns between individuals, then change them to improve interpersonal relationships. TA teaching techniques include contracts, discussions, and specific assignments on how to interact.

One of the most widely discussed approaches to counseling therapy is **crisis therapy** (Redl, 1959). Like other therapies, the focus of crisis therapy is building supportive therapeutic relationships. The point at which crisis therapy begins is an actual life event, not a structured or unstructured therapy session removed from the real world. A key element of crisis therapy is the life space interview, which Redl describes as

> the type of therapy-like interview that a child may need around an incident of stealing from the "kitty" in his club group but that would be held right around the event itself by the group worker in charge of that club, rather than by the child's therapist—even though the same material would probably later come up in therapy too. (pp. 40–41)

The nature of the life space interview depends on its objective. If a teacher simply wants to help a student get through a critical event or crisis, then emotional first aid on the spot is the appropriate strategy; if the intervention target is long-term learning, then a clinical exploitation of life events is appropriate. The student's willingness to take part in the interview as well as the time frame in which it can occur also help determine which strategy a teacher will use.

To deal with the crisis immediately, the teacher should be sympathetic to and understanding of the student's fears, anger, and guilt, but firm about the need for rules and standards of behavior. The objective here is to bring the student back to the task at hand. In clinical therapy, the details of the critical incident are used to teach new behaviors or ways of reacting in similar situations. For example, by pointing out that each time a student calls another student a name, he is likely to get the same reaction, an effective teacher helps the student regulate the future consequences of his behavior. And by offering or having the student suggest new ways to talk to the other student, the teacher helps him develop more appropriate interpersonal skills.

LEARNING STRATEGIES

Students sometimes are trained to follow a step-by-step procedure to acquire teacher-presented content. **Learning strategies training** teaches students how to learn content and how to demonstrate their knowledge. For example, a teacher in Texas taught several of his students to use a three-step paraphrasing procedure represented by the mnemonic RAP (Schumaker, Denton, & Deshler, 1984). Students read a paragraph, ask themselves about the main idea and two supporting details, then put (or paraphrase) the information in their own words.

Learning strategies help students learn content in order to complete teacher-assigned tasks. The strategies are taught to students using direct instructional techniques (Deshler & Schumaker, 1986; Schumaker, Deshler, Alley, & Warner, 1983).

COOPERATIVE LEARNING

Teachers can structure school activities cooperatively, competitively, or individually. In **cooperative learning**, a small group (usually with fewer than six students) works together on an instructional task. Positive interdependence (goals are achieved through the participation of all group members), individual accountability (each participant makes unique contributions to the group's goals), and collaborative skills (communication and decision making) are essential parts of all cooperative learning activities (Johnson & Johnson, 1976).

Mr. Murphy uses cooperative learning to teach social studies. First he breaks an academic unit (say, the Civil War) into several component parts (biographies of key people, major historical events). He then assigns each member of a cooperative learning team one section of the total project (e.g., a ten-page written report, an oral report, a play). Students work independently gathering information, then meet to share their contributions with other team members and to plan the final product. Sometimes final grades are assigned to each student independently; at other times the same grade is awarded to all group members.

Peer-Directed Learning

For many years, questions like "Why can't Johnny read?" have motivated teachers to search for something within their students that causes them to fail. Recently, the concept of *opportunity-to-learn* (the belief that failure is related to the amount of time students actually spend engaged in productive academic activities) has shifted the blame for academic failure from the student to interactions within the classroom. Research finds that students typically spend little time actively engaged in academic tasks, signaling a need to develop instructional methods that can increase opportunities to learn (Delquadri, Greenwood, Whorton, Carta, & Hall, 1986). **Peer tutoring** and **classwide peer tutoring** are two popular types of peer-directed learning which have been shown to increase the time students are actively engaged in learning.

Peer Tutoring

One method that increases instructional opportunities is peer tutoring. In **peer tutoring**, a student is assigned to teach a peer under the supervision of a teacher. One resource room teacher incorporated peer tutoring into her sixth-grade instructional program. Her objectives were to review and practice basic math facts and increase the self-confidence, responsibility, and interpersonal skills of her students. She matched up students from general education third- and fourth-grade classes (who were having difficulties remembering their number facts) with special education students who needed review on the same academic content.

The tutors spent two weeks practicing effective teaching techniques (planning lessons, providing supportive or corrective feedback) before they tutored their students. On Monday and Wednesday of each week, the older students planned their lessons. On Tuesday and Thursday, they tutored for 30 minutes. On Friday, they evaluated their own performance and that of the student they had tutored. Periodically, the classroom teacher evaluated the progress of all the participating students and changed the program as needed.

Classwide Peer Tutoring

Classwide peer tutoring is an instructional alternative in which students supervise one another's responses to academic tasks. One teacher uses classwide peer tutoring twice a week during math. She divides the class into two teams, then pairs the students on each team. Each pair of students creates a set of flashcards by copying single-digit number facts onto index cards. The problem is written on one side of the card, the answer on the other. Then the students actively practice the facts for 20 minutes. During the first ten-minute session, the "teacher" shows the problem sides of the flash cards and the "student" provides the answers. During the second ten-minute session, the paired students swap roles. During both sessions, the "teacher" provides corrective ("No, two plus two equals four") or supportive ("Yes, three plus two equals five") feedback. After the tutoring sessions, the teacher tallies the total points for each team and records the results on a graph in the front of the room.

SOCIAL SKILLS TRAINING

Some teachers take a direct instructional approach to improving students' interpersonal relationships. Critical elements of **social skills training** are a definition of the problem or target behavior, an assessment of the current levels of the problem, and the development and implementation of systematic procedures for teaching new behaviors or improving old ones. Social skills include:

Friendship skills (greetings, joining and leaving activities)

Social maintenance skills (helping, cooperating)

Conflict resolution skills (compromising, persuasion)

Central to social skills training are the four principles of direct instruction: task analysis, modeling expected behavior, corrective and supportive feedback, and independent practice.

3

What Sort of Special Instructional Adaptations Are Available?

Marc Buoniconti was a professional athlete who became paralyzed from the neck down in a football accident. As a dean's list student at the University of Miami, FL, he used a voice-operated computer that managed everything, from answering the telephone to turning on the lights. He exercised daily at the university's medical center, using a high-tech bicycle that electrically stimulated his legs. Buoniconti has proved there is life after football.

—M. Rogers, 1989, p. 66

Students with special needs use voice-operated computers and other instructional adaptations in order to participate in the classroom and in other activities of daily living. These modifications help exceptional students communicate with teachers and other students. Some students may need large-print books to read. Others may need special equipment on their telephones.

Still others need modifications in order to take exams. Instructional adaptations that are commonly used to improve communication and mobility include:

Communication boards

Hearing aids

Amplification systems

Telecommunication devices

Braille

Optacons

Kurzweil reading machines

Calculators

Computers

Test modifications

Guide dogs

Canes

Electronic travel aids

Wheelchairs

Prostheses

COMMUNICATION BOARDS

Communication boards, used by students who cannot speak, have letters and symbols on them. The student points to the letters and symbols in order to communicate. A communication board can be mounted on a wheelchair like a large tray.

HEARING AIDS

Perhaps the most widely known adaptive device is the modern **hearing aid**, a device that amplifies sound. Hearing aids can be worn behind the ear, in the ear, on the body, or in eyeglass frames. Technological advances have made hearing aids smaller, lighter, and more powerful. Audiologists and other hearing specialists usually help families select the type of device that is best suited to meet the needs of the student.

AMPLIFICATION SYSTEMS

Classroom amplification systems also are used to increase the communication abilities of groups of exceptional students. Most amplification systems use a microphone to link the teacher to the students, who wear receivers that often double as personal hearing aids. In one self-contained class of preschoolers with hearing impairments, each student had a small receiver attached around his or her neck; the receiver was connected to a small earplug in one or both ears. The teacher talked to the students using a microphone that hung around her neck. When she spoke to a particular student, she would get his or her attention by touching a shoulder or arm. The teacher and students seemed to have adjusted very well to their adapted form of communication. Amplification systems also are used when students with hearing impairments are integrated in general education classrooms.

TELECOMMUNICATION DEVICES

One way that students who are deaf communicate is by translating verbal messages into written form. The simplest method, of course, is pencil and paper. More sophisticated methods, such as closed-captioned television and telecommunication devices, allow students with deafness to watch TV programs and talk on the telephone. Although you probably have seen the closed-captioned symbol on television [CC], you may not have seen a television equipped for closed captions. The captions are a band of words running across the screen, much like subtitles in a foreign language film, that summarize dialogue or plot.

A **telecommunication device** is a small typewriter with a transmitter/receiver that is connected to a normal telephone by an acoustic coupler. To make a call, you hook your phone to the device and dial another person with a similar device. When the connection is established, a message appears on your screen or printer. Then you type your conversation, which appears on the screen or printer connected to the other person's phone.

Telecommunication devices have broken down long-standing barriers in employment and social interaction for those who have impaired hearing.

BRAILLE

In the early 1800s, Louis Braille developed a system of reading and writing that uses arrangements of six raised dots to represent letters, words, and numbers. Almost 200 years later, braille is still being used by people who are blind or who have severe visual impairments. Although the braille system is complex, blind students can read much faster using it than they can using raised letters of the standard alphabet.

Most students who need braille are introduced to it early in school. They usually are taught a set of contractions rather than letter-by-letter representations of the words they read. Generally it takes students a couple of years to become proficient readers of braille; of course, it usually takes nonexceptional students a couple of years to become proficient readers of print. Students who read braille may learn to write using a **brailler**, a six-keyed device that creates raised-dot words. Older students often use a slate and stylus to punch out braille dots because they are smaller and quieter than a brailler.

OPTACONS

An optacon translates written materials into tactual representations, enabling students who have visual impairments to read.

A miniature camera is moved along a line of print with one hand, while a tactile representation of the letters is felt with the other. The reading rate with an optacon is slow, although some students can read as many as 90 words per minute using one.

KURZWEIL READING MACHINES

Many students with visual impairments use a computer-based device that converts printed words into synthetic English speech. A popular form of this device is the Kurzweil Personal Reader. It has brought independence and self-confidence to many people who have trouble reading any other way.

CALCULATORS

Solar and other portable calculators are common aids for students who have not mastered basic math facts and operations. Calculators can also pique the interest of younger students and provide a vocational link for older students, who typically come across some form of adding machine in their jobs.

COMPUTERS

Computers are increasingly being used to overcome visual, hearing, and physical impairments. Cartwright, Cartwright, and Ward (1989) identify several ways in which computers are being used to help students with visual impairments: Students read print and produce synthetic speech; produce hard-copy braille; read braille, which enables students to do word processing, then output the product in braille; and produce large-print displays.

Computers are helping people with exceptionalities do almost anything (M. Rogers, 1989). A professional musician who is paralyzed, unable to speak or swallow, uses a computer music system to compose and play his work. An architect with severe cerebral palsy, who cannot use his arms and legs, produces elaborate maps using a mouth stick and computer-assisted drafting. For those with extremely limited physical mobility, computers are equipped to be operated just by moving the eyes.

TEST MODIFICATIONS

Both the Individuals With Disabilities Education Act (IDEA) and Section 504 of the Rehabilitation Act assure all people with disabilities the right to a free, appropriate education. This right implies that exceptional students will have the opportunity to complete their education, graduate, and receive a diploma signifying their achievement. Students with special needs are exempted from some statewide testing programs for graduation and promotion purposes. But the idea is not to create second-class degrees; it is to modify testing instruments and procedures so that students with disabilities can demonstrate their achievement. To this end, some states currently allow flexible scheduling, flexible settings, alternative response recording options, revised test formats, and the use of auditory or visual aids for students taking standardized tests.

Flexible scheduling means administering a test during several brief sessions rather than in a single lengthy one. **Flexible settings** mean administering standardized tests to an individual or small group in a resource room or classroom rather than an auditorium. Alternatives for recording answers include marking in the actual test booklet, typing answers, and indicating answers to a test proctor for later transcription to a computer-scored answer sheet. Large-print test booklets and braille tests are used with some exceptional students. Although no portion of a test designed to measure reading skills can be read to a student, narrators and tape-recorded versions of some tests are used with students with seeing problems. Magnifying glasses are another modification for students with visual problems.

GUIDE DOGS

Guide dogs are used by people who are blind to help them move around. They generally are not available to people under age 16; most guide dog schools require that owners be 16 years old because of the responsibility of caring for an animal.

CANES

Several types of canes are used by students with visual impairments to help them get around: long canes, laser canes, orthopedic canes, and folding canes. The most common are long canes—aluminum canes that have a rubber grip, a nylon tip, and a crook. By systematically tapping the cane from side to side to keep track of sidewalks, steps, and walls, students can tell where they are. Laser (light by stimulated emission of radiation) canes emit three narrow beams of infrared light. One of the beams detects objects that are immediately in front of the person; a second, objects at head height; the third, holes and stairs. The cane emits tones that tell the user where objects and holes are in the person's path.

ELECTRONIC TRAVEL AIDS

The Lindsay Russell Model E Pathsounder, Mowat Sensor, and Sonicguide are **electronic travel aids**, devices that send out signals that sense the environment within a range, then translate the information received for the user. The Pathsounder, a boxlike device that weighs about one pound, is chest-mounted and supported by a neck strap. The device emits and receives sonar waves that detect objects in the line of travel. It is used with a long cane as an aid to mobility.

The Mowat Sensor is another travel aid that is used as a supplement to guide dogs and long canes. It is a small hand-held box that locates objects in the person's path of travel. The sensor vibrates when an object is present; the closer the object, the more it vibrates.

The Sonicguide operates much like the Pathsounder and the Mowat Sensor, but it is mounted in a set of eyeglasses. The student also wears an earpiece. The Sonicguide emits pitches and tones that provide information about distance from, and the direction of, objects. It can be used to teach spatial concepts, so it is also used in concept development activities with young students.

WHEELCHAIRS

When students' mobility is limited because they cannot rise from sitting to a standing position or when students who normally use crutches need to carry things while moving around, they generally use wheelchairs. Modern wheelchairs are made of lightweight metal, have durable seats, and four wheels. The two large back wheels have a special rim that helps make the chair move.

PROSTHESES

Some people with physical disabilities use special devices to increase their mobility. Artificial replacements of limbs are known as **prostheses** or **prosthetic devices**. Prostheses allow students to function fully in society.

When model Ivy Hunter was inducted into the International Models Hall of Fame, she joined such modeling legends as Wilhelmina, Naomi Sims, and Cybill Shephard. The honor was in recognition of her personal and professional achievements, achievements in personal courage, and professional commitment, which far exceed those usually demanded of a fashion model.

Ivy Hunter's right leg has been amputated, but she lives a full life:

With a state-of-the-art natural-looking prosthetic leg . . .
Ivy continues to model everything from swimwear
and lingerie to daytime fashions and evening gowns at
photo sessions, runway fashion shows, and in television
commercials. . . . Ivy has learned to snow ski [and] has
garnered several gold and bronze medals in the National
Handicapped Sports and Recreation Association com-
petitions. She also plays tennis, golfs, and water skis.
("Profile: Ivy Hunter," 1988, p. 14)

4

Effective Instruction in Perspective

E ffective teaching is effective teaching, whatever the special needs of the students. General and special educators do the same things: They plan and evaluate instruction and present academic or nonacademic content; they manage classroom instruction; and they spend a portion of the school day involved in other activities (lunch, recess).

Although the components of general and special education instruction are the same, studies tell us that some teachers use methods that are more effective than others. Think of your own school experiences. You probably remember teachers who structured their class presentations around a brilliant selection of supportive media. They knew the best films, had guest lecturers, and made use of well-prepared overheads, slides, and visual aids. Some may even have spun tales of intrigue and mystery about advanced algebra, social studies, and art to capture your attention.

Teachers structure their presentations in unique ways and have students demonstrate their understanding of new material in unique ways. Some teachers are egalitarians: They divide their time equally among subjects and students. They diligently walk around the room, carefully asking each student to read four sentences or recite three lines of a poem or write five multiplication

59

facts on the blackboard. The teaching behaviors of egalitarians are predictable. And students know exactly what they are going to have to do during group instruction.

Of course, not all teachers structure classroom experiences so that each student has a precisely controlled turn. Others keep students on their toes by selecting them to read, recite, write, spell, or otherwise demonstrate a skill in no special order. These teachers are randomizers. With uncanny precision, they are able to duplicate a table of random numbers in their heads and use it as a sequence for calling on students. A particular version of this type of teacher is the one who never calls on students twice (randomization without replacement). You may remember the feeling of relief once you'd performed for a randomizer, the knowledge that you wouldn't be called on again. Both the egalitarian and the randomizer provide an opportunity for each member of the class to take part during a period, but they do so in different ways.

Then there's the humanitarian, the teacher who chooses only those students who know the answers. This gives "the rich" an opportunity to demonstrate their wealth and "the poor" an opportunity not to be embarrassed.

Teachers may share objectives and perform the same basic functions, but they, like the students they teach, are individuals. They have their own ways of delivering instruction, of evaluating instruction, and of interacting with their students. This diversity makes the field of education exciting. It is also the one intangible that makes teaching so rewarding. Perhaps you remember a teacher who made a difference in your educational life.

5

What Have We Learned?

As you complete your study of effective instruction for students with special needs, it may be helpful to review what you have learned. To help you check your understanding of effective instruction for students with special needs, we have listed the key points and key vocabulary for you to review. We have included the Self-Assessment again so you can compare what you know now with what you knew as you began your study. Finally, we provide a few topics for you to think about and some activities for you to do "on your own."

KEY POINTS

All teachers plan, manage, deliver, and evaluate their instruction, whether they are working with students who are gifted, students with disabilities, or students without special needs. More than ever before, teachers are working together to accommodate students with special learning needs, and they are being taught in classroom environments that are as much like general education classrooms as possible. Through combinations of individualized instruction, small- and large-group instruction, teacher- and student-directed instruction, and special instructional methods and approaches, teachers are adapting learning experiences for all students.

- ▣ Effective teaching is effective teaching, whatever the special needs of the students.

- ▣ General and special educators do the same things: They plan and evaluate instruction and present academic or nonacademic content; they manage classroom instruction; and they spend a portion of the school day involved in other activities (lunch, recess).

- ▣ Although the components of general and special education instruction are the same, some teachers use methods that are more effective than others.

- ▣ Effective teachers structure their presentations in unique ways and have students demonstrate their understanding of new material in unique ways.

- ▣ Teachers may share objectives and perform the same basic functions, but they, like the students they teach, are individuals.

- ▣ They have their own ways of planning, managing, delivering, and evaluating instruction.

- ▣ Effective teachers use a variety of approaches to meet the special learning needs of their students, including behavior therapy, precision teaching, ability training, direct instruction, cognitive behavior modification, cognitive skills training, critical thinking, counseling therapy, learning strategies, cooperative learning, peer-directed learning, peer tutoring, classwide peer tutoring, social skills training, and special instructional adaptations (e.g., communication boards, telecommunication devices, test modifications).

- ▣ Diversity in the ways teachers provide effective instruction makes the field of education exciting; it is also the one intangible that makes teaching so rewarding.

Key Vocabulary

Ability training means practicing skills presumed to underlie academic success (e.g., visually tracking from left to right) as a means of improving basic skill (e.g., reading) performance.

Aim line shows the rate of ongoing progress that is necessary for a student to achieve a particular goal.

Attack strategy training is a form of direct instruction in which students are taught the steps of a skill and rules for putting the steps together.

Automaticity means that students complete tasks and demonstrate skills automatically.

Behavior therapy is the process of systematically arranging environmental events to influence behavior.

Brailler is a six-keyed device that creates raised-dot words.

Classwide peer tutoring is an instructional alternative in which students supervise one another's responses to academic tasks.

Client-centered therapy means creating a warm, permissive environment that encourages students to express themselves and to develop their own problem-solving strategies.

Cognitive behavior modification teaches students to use self-statements to improve their performance on academic and other skills.

Contextual variables include where instruction will take place, how long the lesson(s) will be, and who will be in the room during instruction.

Cooperative learning involves a small group (usually with fewer than six students) working together on an instructional task.

Counseling therapy means using interpersonal conversations and carefully structured experiences to influence behaviors.

Crisis therapy involves building supportive therapeutic relationships based on an actual life event, not a structured or unstructured therapy session removed from the real world.

Criterion-referenced tests are used to compare students to standards of mastery relative to the content being measured.

Direct instruction means arranging teaching activities to provide systematic, guided information and precise responses.

Electronic travel aids are devices that send out signals that sense the environment within a range and then translate the information received for the user.

Evaluation is the process by which teachers decide whether the methods and materials they are using are effective—based on students' performance.

Feedback means providing information about a student's performance.

Flexible scheduling means administering a test during several brief sessions rather than in a single lengthy one.

Flexible settings mean administering standardized tests to an individual or small group in a resource room or classroom rather than an auditorium.

Formative evaluation occurs during the process of instruction. The teacher collects data during instruction and uses the data to make instructional decisions.

Hearing aid is a device that amplifies sound.

Instruction is a general term that means providing knowledge in a systematic way.

Learning strategies training teaches students how to learn content and how to demonstrate their knowledge.

Needs assessments are used for determining necessary information or principles for successful completion of a project.

Normative peer comparisons are judgments about the performance of an individual student relative to the average performance of his or her peers.

Norm-referenced tests are used to compare students to each other and to groups on which the test was originally developed.

Operant conditioning is the systematic application and removal of rewards and punishments to increase wanted behaviors and to reduce unwanted behaviors.

Optacons translate written materials into tactual representations so that students who have visual impairments are able to read them.

Pace is how quickly or slowly the class moves through the material. In addition to pace, teachers need to set a ratio of known to unknown material and set standard rates of success.

Peer tutoring involves a student being assigned to teach a classmate or other student under the supervision of a teacher.

Precision teaching involves continuous evaluation of students' progress toward meeting instructional objectives and always focuses on improving skills.

Prostheses or **prosthetic devices** are artificial replacements of limbs.

Reality therapy means helping students identify a problem and ways to rectify it.

Respondent conditioning ties a reflex response to a new stimulus.

Self-contained class is one in which the student spends most of the school day with other students who have disabilities and with at least one special education teacher.

Social skills training is a direct instructional approach to improving students' interpersonal relationships.

Standard behavior chart is used to record a student's progress.

Summative evaluation occurs at the end of instruction, when the teacher administers a test to determine whether the students have met instructional objectives.

Task analysis consists of breaking down a complex task into its component parts.

Teaching is the systematic presentation of content assumed necessary for mastery within a general area of knowledge.

Telecommunication device is a small typewriter with a transmitter/receiver that is connected to a normal telephone by an acoustic coupler.

Transactional analysis involves identifying communication patterns between individuals, then changing them to improve interpersonal relationships.

Self-Assessment 2

A fter you finish this book, check your knowledge of the content covered. Choose the best answer for each of the following questions.

1. Four characteristics of effective instruction are

   a. Planning instruction, teaching, modeling, evaluating

   b. Planning, managing instruction, delivering instruction, evaluating

   c. Modeling examples, delivering instruction, evaluating, revising

   d. Planning instruction, managing behavior, providing feedback, evaluating

2. _____ is the systematic presentation of content assumed necessary for mastery within a general area of knowledge.

   a. Coaching

   b. Presenting

   c. Evaluating

   d. Teaching

3. _____ means making decisions about what information to present, how to present the information, and how to communicate realistic expectations to students.

   a. Planning

   b. Setting goals

    c. Presenting

    d. Modeling

4. Which type of information is gathered by administering criterion-referenced tests?

    a. Knowledge of specific skills that a student should not learn

    b. Intelligence and/or achievement levels

    c. Relative knowledge and grade consistencies

    d. Specific skills or content that a students knows or does not know

5. Which type of information is gathered by administering norm-referenced tests?

    a. Knowledge of specific skills that a student should learn

    b. Intelligence and/or achievement levels

    c. Relative knowledge and grade consistencies

    d. Specific skills or content that a students knows or does not know

6. The process of breaking a complex academic task into its component parts is called _____.

    a. Task analysis

    b. Differentiated instruction

    c. Direct instruction

    d. Task differentiation

7. The educational placement in which a student spends most of the school day with other students who have

disabilities and with at least one special education teacher is called a _____.

a. Self-contained class

b. Special day class

c. Special resource class

d. Special-special class

8. Teachers can make classroom environments positive by _____.

a. Having very strict and consistent rules

b. Using praise to support accomplishments

c. Teaching students to follow their own rules

d. Building strong relationships with other teachers

9. Evaluation that occurs at the end of instruction is called _____.

a. Cumulative evaluation

b. Terminal evaluation

c. Summative evaluation

d. Formative evaluation

10. Evaluation that occurs during instruction is called _____.

a. Cumulative evaluation

b. Terminal evaluation

c. Summative evaluation

d. Formative evaluation

REFLECTION

After you answer the multiple-choice questions, think about how you would answer the following questions:

- What do effective teachers do?
- What are some approaches that have been successful with students with disabilities?
- What is the difference between effective instruction in general and special education classrooms?

Answer Key for Self-Assessments

1. b

2. d

3. a

4. d

5. b

6. a

7. a

8. b

9. c

10. d

On Your Own

☑ Interview a general education classroom teacher who is currently teaching special needs students. Ask the teacher to describe how he or she plans, manages, delivers, and evaluates instruction for the various groups of students in the classroom.

☑ Interview three special education teachers. Ask them to describe how they plan, manage, deliver, and evaluate instruction for the various groups of students in their classrooms.

☑ Observe elementary, middle, and high school teachers working with students with special needs. Note the similarities and differences in what the teachers do during instructional presentations.

☑ Observe general class and special class teachers teaching a student with special needs at various times during the school day. Note any similarities and differences in what these two teachers do.

Resources

WEB SITES

www.interventioncentral.org
Offers free tools and resources to help school staff foster effective learning for all children and youth. This Web site includes tools for intervention team tune-up and general academic strategies as well as resources in specific academic content areas.

www.thegateway.com
The Gateway to Educational Materials gives you access to thousands of educational resources found on various federal, state, university, nonprofit and commercial Internet sites.

BOOKS

Algozzine, B. (1998). *50 simple ways to make teaching more fun.* Longmont, CO: Sopris West Educational Services. This collection of tips for teaching across content areas and promoting responsible student behavior includes guidelines for such activities as palindromes for math practice, bingo for content practice, tickets, awards, lotteries, simple recording systems, and more. Humorous examples and real-life stories illustrate the methods.

Algozzine, B., & Ysseldyke, J. (2003). *Tips for beginning teachers.* Longmont, CO: Sopris West Educational Services. A set of specific tips organized in the same way as this book. Included are additional tips on planning, managing, delivering, and evaluating instruction.

Algozzine, B., Ysseldyke, J. E., & Elliott, J. (1997). *Strategies and tactics for effective instruction.* Longmont, CO: Sopris West Educational Services. This book presents more than 300 practical, research-based tactics in a readily accessible format. Use it to find solutions to instructional challenges in both general and special education classrooms.

Colvin, G., & Lazar, N. (1997). *Effective elementary classroom.* Longmont, CO: Sopris West Educational Services. This book is about organizing a classroom for success and keeping behavior problems to a minimum by using practical classroom management procedures. It provides the nitty-gritty details for organizing classroom space, establishing routines, managing instruction, preventing and managing problem behavior, establishing expectations, using groups in instruction, and working with other school personnel.

Kemp, K., & Fister, S. (2002). *TGIF: But what will I do on Monday?* Longmont, CO: Sopris West Educational Services. More than 250 proven techniques to help educators cope with skill deficits in their students. Teachers look up a specific challenge and find the solution that best fits it. The resource is organized into sections on teacher-directed instruction, guided practice activities, independent practice activities, and final measurement (hence the acronym TGIF).

Lambert, M., & Algozzine, B. (2003). *Strategies that make learning fun.* Longmont, CO: Sopris West Educational Services. More than 40 easy-to-implement learning strategies in reading, writing, math, study skills, and social skills. Tips on how to adapt instruction to the needs of individual students.

ORGANIZATIONS

Association for Supervision and Curriculum Development (ASCD)

Founded in 1943, ASCD has 150,000 members. It is a professional organization of supervisors, curriculum coordinators, directors, and others interested in school improvement at all levels of education. ASCD provides professional development and training in curriculum and supervision; disseminates information; and encourages research, evaluation, and theory development. ASCD, 1250 Pitt St., Alexandria, VA 22314–1403.

References

Algozzine, B., Ysseldyke, J. E., & Elliott, J. (1997). *Strategies and tactics for effective instruction.* Longmont, CO: Sopris West Educational Services.

Asch, A. (1989). Has the law made a difference? What some disabled students have to say. In D. Lipsky & A. Gartner (Eds.), *Beyond separate education: Quality education for all* (pp. 181–205). Baltimore: Brookes.

Bloom, B. (Ed.). (1956). *Taxonomy of educational objectives. Handbook I: Cognitive domain.* New York: McKay.

Cartwright, G., Cartwright, C., & Ward, M. (1989). *Educating special learners* (3rd ed.). Belmont, CA: Wadsworth.

Cartwright, P. G. & Shapiro, W. L. (1995). *Educating special learners* (4th ed.). Belmont, CA: Wadswroth.

Clark, B. (1983). *Growing up gifted* (2nd ed.). Columbus, OH: Merrill.

Clark, B. (2001). *Growing up gifted: Developing the potential of children at home and at school* (6th ed.). Upper Saddle River, NJ: Prentice Hall.

Delquadri, J., Greenwood, C., Whorton, D., Carta, J., & Hall, V. (1986). *Exceptional Children, 52,* 542–583.

Deshler, D., & Schumaker, J. (1986). Learning strategies: An instructional alternative for low achieving adolescents. *Exceptional Children, 52,* 583–590.

Entwistle, N., Skinner, D., Entwistle, D., & Orr, S. (2000). Conceptions and beliefs about "good teaching": An integration of contrasting research areas. *Higher Education Research and Development, 19,* 19–26.

Ethell, R. G., & McMeniman, M. M. (2000). Unlocking the knowledge in action of an expert practitioner. *Journal of Teacher Education, 51,* 87–101.

Glasser, W. (1965). *Reality therapy.* New York: Harper & Row.

Glasser, W. (1989). *Reality therapy: A new approach to psychiatry* (Reissue ed.). New York: Harper Paperbacks.

Good, T., & Brophy, J. (1984). *Looking in classrooms* (3rd ed.). New York: Harper & Row.

Good, T. L., & Brophy, J. E. (2002). *Looking in classrooms* (9th ed.). Boston: Allyn & Bacon.

Ho, A. S. P. (2000). A conceptual change approach to staff development: A model for programme design. *International Journal for Academic Development, 5,* 87–101.

Johnson, D. W., & Johnson, R. T. (1976). *Learning together and alone: Cooperative, competitive, and individualistic learning* (4th ed.). Boston: Allyn & Bacon.

Johnson, D. W., & Johnson, R. T. (1998). *Learning together and alone: Cooperative, competitive, and individualistic learning* (5th ed.). Boston: Allyn & Bacon.

Kember, D., Kwan, K. P., & Ledesma, J. (2001). Conceptions of good teaching and how they influence the way adults and school leavers are taught. *International Journal of Lifelong Education, 202,* 393–404.

Lloyd, J. (1980). Academic instruction and cognitive behavior modification: The need for attack strategy training. *Exceptional Education Quarterly, 1,* 53–63.

Ornstein, A. C., & Levine, D. U. (1993). *Foundations of education* (5th ed.). Boston: Houghton Mifflin.

Ornstein, A.C. Levine, D.U. Gutek, G., & Lawlor, J.C. (2004). *Foundations of education* (9th ed.). Boston: Houghton Mifflin.

Profile: Ivy Hunter. (1988, November/December). *A Positive Approach,* 14.

Redl, F. (1959). The concept of the lifespace interview. *American Journal of Orthopsychiatry, 29,* 1–18.

Rogers, C. (1951). *Client-centered therapy.* Boston: Houghton Mifflin.

Rogers, M. (1989, April 24). Technology: More than wheelchairs. *Newsweek,* 66–67.

Samuelowicz, K., & Bain, J. D. (2001). Revisiting academics' beliefs about teaching and learning. *Higher Education, 41,* 299–325.

Schumaker, J., Denton, P., & Deshler, D. (1984). *The paraphrasing strategy.* Lawrence: University of Kansas Institute for Research on Learning Disabilities.

Schumaker, J., Deshler, D., Alley, G., & Warner, M. (1983). Toward the development of an intervention model for learning disabled adolescents: The University of Kansas Institute. *Exceptional Education Quarterly, 4,* 45–70.

Wang, M. C. (1989). Adaptive instruction: An alternative for accommodating student diversity through the curriculum. In D. Lipsky & A. Gartner (Eds.), *Beyond separate education: Quality education for all* (pp. 99–119). Baltimore: Brookes.

Wittrock, M. C. (1986). Handbook of research on teaching (3rd ed.) New York: Macmillan.

Yost, D. S., Sentner, S. M., & Forlenza-Bailey, A. (2000). An examination of the construct of critical reflection: Implications for teacher education programming in the 21st century. *Journal of Teacher Education, 51,* 39–49.

Ysseldyke, J. E., & Algozzine, B. (1990). *Introduction to special education.* Boston: Houghton Mifflin.

Index

Note: Numbers in **Bold** followed by a colon [:] denote the book number within which the page numbers are found.

**CORWIN
PRESS**

The Corwin Press logo—a raven striding across an open book—represents the union of courage and learning. Corwin Press is committed to improving education for all learners by publishing books and other professional development resources for those serving the field of PreK–12 education. By providing practical, hands-on materials, Corwin Press continues to carry out the promise of its motto: **"Helping Educators Do Their Work Better."**